MW00885111

Let us Introduce you to Ethel Lou

In this book, you will find recipes from one of the best cooks of all time. You will also find stories from people that not only loved her recipes, but cherished her as a person even more. You will see pictures that were chosen to go with certain recipes or short stories for specific reasons. You will also see pictures that were added to the book just simply because they are some of our favorite pictures of her and the people she loved so dearly. You will see lots of cardinals because that was her favorite bird. She collected cardinals for many years. You will also see red flowers all throughout this book because she loved red and she loved flowers. She made the statement one time "if we have jobs in Heaven, I hope I get to work in a flower garden".

This book was written and inspired by:
Crystal, Mikayla, and Ashleigh

Crystal is Ethel Lou's daughter. She wanted to create a book that would honor her Mom and allow everyone that knew her to hold onto a few pieces of her for many years to come. One book can't possibly summarize all of the hundreds of recipes, thousands of stories, and millions of memories, but Crystal wanted to use this book as a way of highlighting a little of each.

Mikayla and Ashleigh are Ethel Lou's granddaughters. They also wanted to create a book that would showcase what a special Nana they had. Their Nana meant the world to them and this book will hopefully give you an idea of just how special she was.

Throughout this book you will see "Mom" and you will see "Nana" because that's what she was to the three women that put heart and soul into this book.

How it all began.....

Two wonderful people, born on the same day two years apart, fell in love.

Howard Fender was born on March 29, 1918 to Fildon Fender and Sally Lewis Fender. Sally passed away when Howard was 15 months old to tuberculosis. Fildon then married Annie Phillips Fender.

Pearl Faye Edwards was born on March 29, 1920 to Reverend Emory Edwards and Minnie Adkins Edwards.

Howard and Pearl were married on December 24, 1936. This is where our "Host of Fenders" began. Howard and Pearl were wonderful Christian examples to their family and all who knew them.

As Howard and Pearl's love grew, so did their family. They were blessed with five wonderful children; Ezra, Ethel "Lou", Norma Jean, Larry James, and Darius Fender.

Ezra was born on October 15, 1937. Ezra married Wanda Ray and they were blessed with Mona Lisa, Sherri Lea, Randall Scott, and Don Allison Fender "Donnie". Donnie passed away after only two days on this earth.

Ethel "Lou" was born on February 10, 1941. Lou married Junior Ray "JR" Bradford and they were blessed with Patrick Ray and Crystal Anne Bradford, and also identical twin sons, Kelly Joe and Keith Jason, whom they lost at birth.

Norma Jean was born on July 26, 1943. Norma married Don Ramsey and they were blessed with Beverly Rene' "Tina", and Jada Nicole Ramsey. Later in years, Don passed away and Norma married Alden Edwards.

Larry James was born on September 4, 1949. Larry married Sandra McFalls and they were blessed with David Michael and Joshua James Fender.

Darius was born on June 10, 1952. Darius married Hope Robinson and they were blessed with Glendon David Fender.

Their kids married and had kids of their own whom married and had kids of their own. We have added some and some have been taken away, and some got to be part by name only, but this is how the story of the "Host of Fenders" began.

By the help of the Lord, we try to move forward and carry on the traditions and keep doing the things we were taught in the little white house with the red roof on Little Creek...not just because this is my family, but oh how blessed I am to be a part.

Crystal

The house that built us

> But as for me and my house, we will serve the Lord.
> Joshua 24:15

All because two people fell in love

Howard and Pearl Fender "Ma and Pa"

Host of "Fenders"

Some photos of the Fender crew

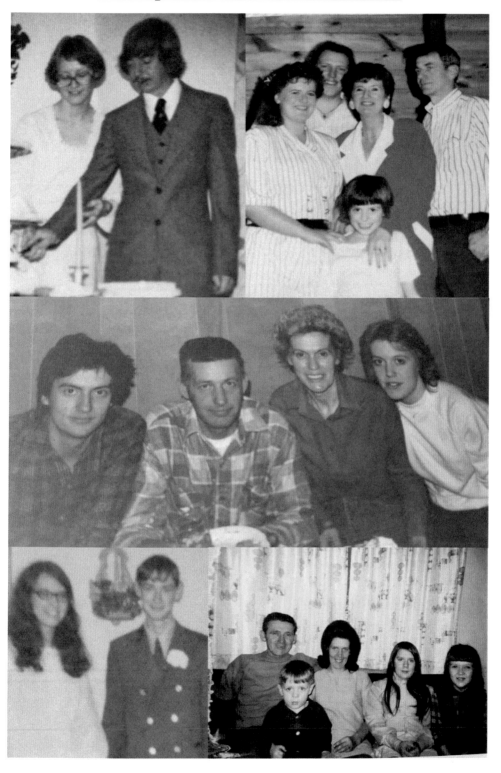

In loving memory of....

Staff Sargent Donald Ramsey
Born on July 28, 1940 and passed
away on March 27, 2004.
Don was married to
Lou's sister Norma.

Wanda Lee Ray Fender
Born on July 5, 1942 and passed
away on January 17, 2000.
Wanda was married to
Lou's brother Ezra.

Ma Pearl's Mom and Dad
Reverend Emory and Minnie Edwards

Crystal and her Great-Aunt Ruth

Pa Howard with his
step-mom (Ma Annie) and his sister Ruth

Ma Pearl with some of her siblings

Lou's in-laws
(Junior Ray's parents)
Joe and Nell Bradford

Let me tell you the story about Mom's in-laws. Preacher Joe Bradford was born on March 18, 1920 to William and Nora Radford Bradford. Nellie Jane Hensley was born on November 28, 1920 to Turner and Birdie Ann Tipton Hensley. Joe and Nellie (Nell) were married on June 15, 1940. Joe and Nell had three children; Junior Ray, Albert Dean (Eb), and Judy Ann Bradford.

Junior Ray "JR" Bradford was born on June 10, 1941. He married Ethel Lou Fender on October 20, 1962. Their children were Patrick Ray and Crystal Anne Bradford, as previously mentioned in the "Fender" story. They also had twin boys (Kelly Joe and Keith Jason) whom passed away at birth.

Albert Dean Bradford "Eb" was born on March 8, 1945. He married Georgia Ann Mains. They were blessed with Timothy Leon Bradford, Sam Bradford, George Staci and Stephanie Maxine McBride.

Judy Ann Bradford was born on June 5, 1951. She married Eddie Robinson on June 2, 1969. They were blessed with Rebecca Ann and Amanda "Mandy" Deniell Robinson.

There are great memories of our younger years together.

Crystal

Some photos of the Bradford crew

The younger years of the Bradford crew

More photos of the Bradford crew

A few more of the Bradford crew

Coconut Pie
Ma Pearl's recipe passed down to Nana

Pie Ingredients

1 cup sugar
5 tablespoons flour
1 cup coconut
2 cups milk
3 eggs
4 tablespoons butter

Meringue "Cow Slobber"

3 egg whites
6 tablespoons sugar
(beat until stiff peaks form)

Nana used to add a teaspoon of coconut flavoring to her pie filling mixture, (it was her little secret).

Directions

Mix all together. Cook mixture on stovetop for 5-7 minutes. Pour into a pre-baked pie crust. Top with homemade meringue. Sprinkle more coconut on top. Bake at 450 degrees until browned.

Lou, Norma, Larry, Ezra

Nana would make this pie lots of times when her siblings were at Ma and Pa's house mowing and cleaning.

Butterscotch Cream Pie

Ingredients

3/4 cup brown sugar
3 tablespoons flour
1 tablespoon corn starch
1/4 teaspoon salt
1-1/2 cups milk
3 egg yolks, beaten
2 tablespoons butter
1 teaspoon vanilla
1 pie crust

Directions

Combine the sugar, flour, corn starch, and salt in top of double boiler. Mix with wooden spoon. Blend in milk gradually. Add egg yolks and butter. Place over rapidly boiling water. Cook until thick and smooth for 7 minutes, stirring constantly. Remove from heat then add vanilla. Stir until smooth and blended. Pour hot filling into a pie shell. Cover with meringue and bake in oven on 300 degrees for 20 minutes.

What I miss the most is when we would cut grass and Lou would cook lunch, then the four of us would sit on the porch and talk and laugh. She was a great sister.
Larry Fender

Larry, Norma, Lou, Ezra

Chocolate Gravy

Nana created many memories with this dish!

Ingredients

1 cup sugar
1 cup water
1 cup milk
4 tablespoons flour
3 tablespoons cocoa

Directions

Bring water and milk to a rolling boil.
Add sugar, flour, and cocoa.
Stir constantly until thickened.
Serve with butter and hot biscuits.

Nana and Brayden

Nana and Ashleigh

<u>Chocolate Gravy Continued....Ashleigh's Memory</u>

It's funny how the simple things seem to stick in my mind and mean the most to me, those little moments we shared, going about an average day with average tasks, but that hold the most precious place in my heart.

The rest of the world isn't hardly up yet, the birds just barely out of the nest, the sun is peeking over the tops of the mountains. It's all very quiet, very peaceful. In a house on Little Creek, there is a kitchen light on above the sink. The rest of the house is dim. I know because I lay sleeping on the couch. Papaw Jr. comes through the house sneaking by, eager to stick his fingertip in my ear and whisper, "Ash"! Well, it was peaceful, I said.

Papaw worked for Eastman Kodak Company in Tennessee and had quite a drive ahead of him every morning. Nana rose early with him to make sure he had a full stomach and a packed lunch for the work hours ahead of him.

I stir a little on top of the cushions, thanks to my wake-up call. But what brings me to my senses is those heavenly sounds and smells coming from the kitchen. Warm and buttery biscuits, sweet cocoa powder fills the air and a strong distinct smell of coffee on the stove. I hear Nana and Papaw quietly whispering, the kettle on the stove starting to whistle, the wooden spoon clinks against the metal pot. It's all very familiar, it happens this way every time I stay.

I convince myself it'll be well worth it to get up and shuffle my feet to the kitchen, the light hurts my eyes. I plop down at the table in "my seat", the one with my back to the stove. Papaw is to my left and Nana to my right and I hear "Morning Ashy!" Papaw pokes at me but it's too early for this nonsense. I grunt a little. Nana jumps up and starts making me a plate. I watch her crumble my biscuit on top of the same ole apple patterned plate, a healthy dollop of butter on top, then she spoons the chocolate gravy over the two. It's making my mouth water. She fills my glass with milk and we all dig in. After I've stuffed myself to the brim with a biscuit or a few, I'm getting sleepy. Papaw says his goodbyes and I crawl back under my quilt on the couch. I have a few more hours of sleep calling my name and then we get up and me and Nana do it all over again, a second helping of homemade memories.

Now looking back, I know it was well worth it.

Ashleigh

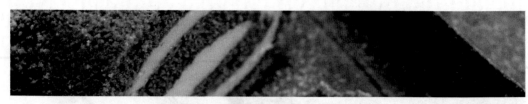

Pumpkin Cake Roll

Cake Ingredients

3 eggs
1 cup sugar
2/3 cup pumpkin (canned or fresh)
1 tsp. lemon juice
3/4 cup self-rising flour
2 tsp. cinnamon
1 tsp. ginger

Note: you can replace the cinnamon and ginger with pumpkin pie spice if you prefer.

Filling Ingredients

1 cup powdered sugar
6 oz. cream cheese
4 tablespoons butter
1/2 tsp. vanilla
(beat together until thick then set aside to spread on pumpkin roll)

Directions

Mix all cake ingredients together then pour onto a greased and floured cookie sheet. Bake at 375 degrees for 10-15 minutes. Turn out onto a towel covered in powdered sugar, roll up, cool for about 2 hours. Unroll and spread with filling. Roll back up and chill then slice. Ready to serve.

<u>Pumpkin Cake Roll....continued</u>

For almost the past 15 years, we have been having a Christmas gathering, usually the weekend before Christmas, at my house. All are invited - family, friends, and anyone that wants to come. We always have wonderful food and fellowship! We usually start the night with Crick's (Crystal's) famous lasagna. We have salad, bread, and every kind of appetizer that you can think of. Everyone just brings a dish and it is always delicious.

First, let me say, Lou Lou (Nana) never just brought one dish! There was always several of my favorite things; pumpkin roll, fried pies, sour dough bread, peanut butter fudge, and cheesecake. Now let me tell you about these desserts. You cannot have a gathering without Lou Lou's sweets. All of my life, Lou Lou would try to teach me how to make things. As a little girl, I remember her letting me watch and help her. As I got older, she would write out the recipes for me. I know she probably got tired of me pestering her about why mine didn't turn out like hers, but mine will never taste as good as Lou Lou's. She had a special touch that the rest of us do not have. She baked with LOVE!

I always looked forward to her pumpkin roll. I loved it. It was so good and rich with all the gooey cream cheese in the middle. If you have had it before...then you know! It would always get gone quickly, so I learned to get me a piece and hide it on top of the refrigerator for the next day.

Lou Lou was one of the Godliest women I knew. She has prayed for me and my babies as long as I can remember. We have dug in the dirt and swapped flowers and had conversations on the goodness of God. Thank you Lou Lou for a lifetime of precious memories.

Becky

Mandy, Lou,
Becky, & Crystal

Pistachio Cake
This cake is April's Favorite

Cake Ingredients

1 box (18.25 oz) white cake mix
1 package (3.4 oz) instant pistachio pudding mix
3 eggs
1 cup vegetable oil
1 can (12 oz) lemon-lime soda (such as 7-up)

Frosting Ingredients

1 package (3.4 oz) instant pistachio pudding mix
1-1/2 cups milk
1 container (8 oz) frozen whipped topping (thawed)
1/4 cup chopped pistachio nuts (to garnish)

Directions

Preheat oven to 350 degrees. Coat two (9-inch) round cake pans with cooking spray then line with waxed paper then spray again. In a large bowl, beat: cake mix, pudding mix, eggs, vegetable oil, and soda on medium speed for 4 minutes (scraping sides after 2 minutes). Equally divide batter between cake pans. Bake for 35 minutes or until a toothpick comes out clean. Cool cake layers in pans for 15 minutes, then turn out onto a rack and cool completely.

Prepare the frosting: In a large bowl, beat pudding mix and milk for 2 minutes. Fold in whipped topping. Place one cake layer on a plate and spread with one cup of frosting. Place remaining layer on top then frost top and sides with remaining frosting. Garnish with chopped nuts. Refrigerate for at least one hour before serving. Store in refrigerator.

Pistachio Cake Continued....April's Memory

It's hard to pick a favorite recipe when it comes to Nana's cooking. Nana made everything perfect and with so much love. This "green cake" stands out to me as when she learned it was one of my favorites, she would always make a point to fix it. You never left Nana's hungry!

April

Peanut Butter Fudge

This fudge is a favorite chosen by many!

Ingredients

3 cups sugar
3/4 cup milk
1-1/2 sticks butter
1 small jar marshmallow cream
1-1/2 cups peanut butter

Directions

Mix sugar, milk, butter in a pot then bring to a boil. Boil 5 minutes then remove from stove. Stir in peanut butter and marshmallow cream. Cool, slice, and serve.

Levi loved his Nana's peanut butter fudge and he also loved her kitty "Bandit"!

Nana, Levi, and Bandit

<u>**Peanut Butter Fudge Continued....**</u>

Of all the recipes Mom had and all the things she made, fudge was a favorite of most. I have bought different types of fudge in many different candy stores, but none ever compared to my Mom's. It was always the perfect consistency being so smooth and soft. It was never hard and grainy. She started out with chocolate, butterscotch, and peanut butter, then later added dreamsicle and salted caramel. It was such a treat!

Crystal

Sandra always loved Nana's peanut butter fudge as well! She and Nana were sisters-in-law, but were as close as sisters.

Sandra and Lou

Levi and Sandra

Seeing the picture of us sitting on the porch reminds me of the last time we sat on the porch and talked. At a gathering last summer, everyone went up the road for a while. Lou didn't want to go so I stayed with her. We laughed and talked for about an hour. She wanted to talk about Patrick and some of the funny things he did and said. I'm so thankful we had that time to talk. We also talked about how we were more like sisters than sisters-in-law. I loved her dearly and miss her very much. I know I will be seeing her again and we can sit on the porch and talk again.

Sandra Fender

Part 1: Sourdough Bread Starter

Ingredients for Starter
1 package dry yeast
1/2 cup lukewarm water
2 tablespoons sugar
2 cups warm water
2-1/2 tablespoons all-purpose flour

Ingredients for Potato Feed
3/4 cup sugar
3 tablespoons instant potatoes
1 cup warm water

Directions

Mix yeast with 1/2 cup warm water. Mix sugar with 2 cups warm water and flour. Add yeast mixture to sugar mixture. Let set in a glass jar covered with a cloth for 5 days.

Next, put the initial sourdough starter (above) in refrigerator for 3-5 days. Take out and feed with this mixture: 3/4 cup sugar, 3 tablespoons instant potatoes, 1 cup warm water. Mix well and add to starter. Let starter stand out of fridge all day (8-12 hours) or until very bubbly. Remove 1 cup to make bread and return remaining to the fridge. Keep in fridge for 3-5 days and feed again. (If not making bread after feeding, throw away 1 cup, but it may be fed 2-3 times before using for any bread (This is to avoid depleting your starter).

This picture includes: Randall, Sherri, Patrick, Tina, Crystal, Ma Pearl, and Lisa.

Randall, Sherri, and Lisa are Ezra and Wanda's three children and they always loved this bread!

Part 2: Baking the Sourdough Bread

Ingredients

1/3 cup sugar
1/2 cup corn oil
1 tablespoon salt
1 cup potato fed starter (previous page)
1-1/2 cups warm water
6 cups white bread flour

Directions

In a large bowl, blend sugar, oil, salt, potato starter, water, and flour. This makes a stiff batter.

Grease another bowl, add dough and turn it over so that it is greased on all sides. Lightly cover with foil and let stand overnight (do not refrigerate).

Next morning, punch down the dough. Knead a little. Divide into three parts and knead each part 8-10 times on a floured board. Put into a greased loaf pan and brush with oil. Cover with waxed paper or a tea towel. Let rise until doubled (4-5 hours or all day since the dough rises very slowly).

Uncover dough and bake in a 350 degree oven for 30-35 minutes or until bread tests done. Remove from pan and brush with butter. Cool on rack. Wrap well and store. Refrigerate. Bread may be frozen.

This group went Christmas caroling at Lou's in 2022

Dreamsicle Fudge

Ingredients

1-1/2 sticks margarine
2/3 cup cream
3 cups sugar
1 (12 oz) package vanilla chips
1 (7 oz) jar marshmallow cream
2-1/2 teaspoons orange flavoring
12 drops yellow food coloring
9 drops red food coloring

Directions

Mix margarine, cream, and sugar in a sauce pan. Bring to a boil. Boil until it reaches soft ball stage (6-7 minutes). Remove from stove then add marshmallow cream and vanilla chips and mix well. Set aside 1 cup of this mixture. To remaining mixture in pan, add flavoring and food colorings. Pour into a buttered 9 x 13 glass pan. Take the 1 cup reserved mixture and pour over mixture in pan. Swirl with a knife. Cool, slice, and serve.

On the left....Nana's brother Darius with the dreamsicle fudge on his plate.

On the right....Nana with her nephew Glendon.

Dreamsicle Fudge Continued....

Michael Peterson

Mike and Mama

This is Mike, Mama's son-in-law. What a special bond they had. Mama always bragged about how good Mike was to her. He was always there to help her any way he could. He helped her out with projects around the house. He also loved to buy her stuff and surprise her. She would always send him things that she knew he liked if she had leftovers. He loved many things she made including coconut pie, fried chicken, peanut butter fudge, and the dreamsicle fudge was also one of his favorites.

Creamy Hash Browns

Ingredients

1 bag (32 oz.) frozen hash brown potatoes
1 can cream of chicken soup
1 cup shredded cheese
1 cup sour cream
1 small onion (chopped)
1-1/2 sticks butter
1/4 teaspoon paprika
2 cups corn flakes (crushed)

Directions

Mix first seven ingredients together well.
Bake at 350 degrees for 30 minutes.
Top with crushed corn flakes.
Continue baking for 20-30 minutes.

Me and my precious Mom

Peach Delight

Ingredients

1st Layer
2 cups self-rising flour
1-1/2 sticks butter (melted)
1 cup pecans

2nd Layer
1 (8 oz) block cream cheese
2-1/2 cups powdered sugar
1 (8 oz) container cool whip

3rd Layer
4 cups sliced peaches

4th Layer
1 cup sugar
4 tablespoons flour
4 tablespoons peach Jello
1 cup water

Directions

For Layer #1:
Mix all ingredients together and spread into a 9 x 13 pan. Bake on 350 degrees for 15-20 minutes. Let cool completely.

For Layer #2:
Mix all ingredients together and spread over cooled crust.

For Layer #3:
Place all peaches over top of layer 2.

For Layer #4:
Mix all ingredients together and cook in a saucepan until thick and clear. Cool this mixture completely. Pour cooled mixture over peaches.

*This is better if it is refrigerated overnight.
*Use a graham cracker crust in place of the first layer if you prefer.

<u>Mikayla's Memory</u>

Nana (Ethel Lou) shared her mountain traditions with several NC State college students. The dishes of "ramps" and "killed lettuce" are specific to Western North Carolina, so Nana brought Yancey County to Raleigh by cooking for me and my college roommates. Nana's friend Maggie and my Mom (Crystal) were there too and helped prepare the meal. Ramps are a strong version of an onion that grows in the wild (not just something you used to get off an exit). Ramps are usually served mixed in with fried taters or eggs and some people even enjoy them raw. Branch lettuce can be found near small bodies of water or be substituted with bib lettuce or spring mix. It gets its name by pouring fat back or bacon grease over the lettuce to "kill" it. Although neither dish is considered the most healthy, they sure are delicious.

Not many grandparents over the age of 70 would ride 5 hours to see their grandchild at college, let alone to cook for them, but that was Nana. She always put others before herself no matter the aches or pains that might ail someone traveling that far. Nana always put her family first and was willing to do whatever to make her grandkids happy. Her love was not just words, it was actions. Nana came to visit me several times while I was in college. She came to a BBQ fundraiser for my sorority along with her sister Norma and my Mom. They visited me at the small ruminant unit to see the goats and sheep and came to see me walk across stage as a first generation college student. Nana was proud of all her grandkids and their accomplishments but wanted them to never forget where they came from and most of all to follow the Lord in every aspect of their lives.

Mikayla

Me, Nana, & Mom

Me, Nana, Mom, & Aunt Norma

Me and my college roommates

Nana and her friend Maggie

Sisters

I loved my sister with all my heart. I'm so glad God put us together in a loving home. I'll never forget our good times growing up and our teenage years. I remember our Kool-Aid parties and Mom and Dad letting us have friends over. She always got the good-looking guys. Then came the drivers licenses and cars. She loved cars, especially her 59' Chevy. She finally let me drive it to school my senior year. I'll never forget her going through Davis Produce Stand....thank goodness we had praying parents. I have to think of the good times and the fun we had. My heart breaks when I think of her leaving me.
Norma Jean

Lou on the left, Norma on the right

Deep Dish Fruit Pie

Ingredients

1 cup sugar
1 cup flour
1 cup milk
1 stick butter
3 teaspoons baking powder
1 quart sweetened fruit

Directions

Preheat oven to 350 degrees.
Melt butter in a 9 x 13 dish in the
preheated oven.
Mix together the milk, sugar, flour,
and baking powder.
Pour batter over melted butter.
Pour sweetened fruit over the batter.
Bake on 350 degrees for 30 minutes.

Prune Cake

This is Ms. Wilson's Recipe

Cake Ingredients

3 eggs
1 cup Wesson oil
1-1/2 cups sugar
2 cups self-rising flour
1-1/2 cups cooked prunes
1 teaspoon cinnamon
1 teaspoon nutmeg
1 teaspoon allspice
2 teaspoons baking soda
2 teaspoons vanilla
1 cup buttermilk
3 egg whites (beaten)

Sauce Ingredients

1 cup sugar
1/2 teaspoon baking soda
1 teaspoon vanilla
1 cup buttermilk
1/2 stick butter
1 tablespoon syrup

Directions

Mix all cake ingredients together. Pour into a 9 x 13 greased pan. Bake on 325 degrees for 40 minutes.

Allow the cake to cool, then prepare the sauce.

For the sauce: Place all sauce ingredients in a pot and mix well. Bring to a boil and let boil for 2 minutes. Pour over warm cake.

Nana and her Niece Lisa   Lisa and Emery

Made With Love

Never in my life did I think at 53 years old, I would be the only one left of my initial family unit. Some days it is extremely hard to understand or not ask "why", and some days with the help of the Lord, I am able to put one foot in front of the other and try to move forward. I am so thankful for the memories I have.

Come with me and I will take you back. We may not have been rich, but we had Jesus and so much love for one another. When our birthday rolled around, it was a big deal to Mom. She always cooked our favorite meal and made our favorite cake. Daddy's favorite was red velvet cake, Patrick's was strawberry jello cake, and mine was orange crush cake. Mom's cakes were the best. They were made with love!

Crystal

Me and Daddy

Dad and Mom when they got married

Mom and Patrick

Fruit Pizza

This was Mom's personal favorite!

Ingredients

4 cups Corn Flakes cereal (crushed to 1 cup)
2 tablespoons sugar
2 tablespoons margarine (softened)
2 tablespoons light corn syrup
2 packages (8 oz. each) light cream cheese (softened)
1 jar (7 oz.) marshmallow cream
3 cups sliced fruit (fresh or canned)

Directions

Preheat oven to 350 degrees. In a medium-sized bowl, combine corn flake cereal, sugar, margarine, and corn syrup. Press mixture evenly and firmly in bottom of a 12-inch pizza pan. Bake for 5 minutes or until lightly browned then cool completely. Combine cream cheese and marshmallow cream. Spread over crust. Arrange fruit over cream cheese mixture. Chill for 1 hour or until firm.

Mom didn't want us to spend money to buy her a birthday cake so she would say "just make my favorite Crystal". She was referring to the fruit pizza!

Mom's 77th Birthday

Red Velvet Cake

This cake was Daddy's favorite!

Cake Ingredients

1/2 cup shortening
1-1/2 cups sugar
2 tablespoons cocoa
1/2 teaspoon salt
1 teaspoon soda
2-1/2 cups plain flour
1 teaspoon vanilla
2 eggs
2 oz. red food coloring
1 tablespoon vinegar
1 cup buttermilk

Frosting Ingredients

1 cup milk
5 teaspoons flour
1 cup butter
1 teaspoon vanilla
1 cup sifted powdered sugar

Directions

Cream shortening and sugar. Add eggs one at a time beating after each addition. Add food coloring and cocoa. Sift flour and salt together and add alternately with buttermilk. Stir soda into vinegar then quickly add and stir. Bake in 3 layer cake pans at 350 degrees for 30-35 minutes.

For the Frosting:

Cook the milk and flour together until thick and then cool in the refrigerator.
Add the butter, vanilla, and powdered sugar to the cooled mixture a little at a time. Spread onto the cooled cake.

<u>Red Velvet Cake continued....</u>

My Sweet Daddy....Junior Ray

My Daddy and my daughter Mikayla

<u>Strawberry Jello Cake</u>
This cake was Patrick's favorite!

<u>Cake Ingredients</u>
1 box white cake mix
1 box strawberry jello mix
1/2 cup warm water
4 eggs
1 cup Wesson oil
1/2 cup mashed strawberries

<u>Frosting Ingredients</u>
1 box powdered sugar
1 stick of butter (melted)
2-4 tablespoons milk
1 container of store-bought icing:
(strawberry or vanilla)
1/4 cup mashed strawberries
*add food coloring if you want

<u>Directions</u>
Dissolve jello mix in warm water. In a separate bowl mix together: cake mix, eggs, oil, then add in the jello mixture. Blend well, then add strawberries and stir. Bake at 350 degrees. Let cool completely. Prepare the frosting by blending all icing ingredients until smooth. Add the milk a little at a time until it's the consistency you like.
Spread the frosting over cooled cake.

Mikayla, Crystal, Patrick, Ashleigh

Patrick and Mom

Orange Crush Cake

This cake was Crystal's favorite!

Cake Ingredients

1 box white cake mix
1-1/4 cups orange soda (cold)
1/4 cup canola oil
2 large eggs

Frosting Ingredients

1 cup orange soda (cold)
2 envelopes Dream Whip
1 small can mandarin oranges
(drained) for the top

Directions

Preheat oven to 350 degrees. Lightly grease a 9 x 13 cake pan with cooking spray and set aside. Combine the cake mix, 1-1/4 cups orange soda, canola oil, and eggs in a large bowl. Whisk on low speed for 30 seconds and then increase speed to medium for 2 minutes. Pour batter into prepared pan and bake for 30-35 minutes or until a toothpick comes out clean. Let cake cool completely.

For the frosting: In a large bowl, beat together 1 cup of orange soda and 2 envelopes of Dream Whip on low speed for 30 seconds and then on medium until soft peaks form. Spread on cooled cake then garnish with mandarin orange segments.

Mom and Me

Blowing out my birthday candles

Chocolate Dumplings

Sauce Ingredients

3/4 cup packed brown sugar
1/4 cup baking cocoa
1 tablespoon cornstarch
dash of salt
2 cups water
2 tablespoons butter

Dumpling Ingredients

1-1/4 cups all-purpose flour
2 teaspoons baking powder
1/2 teaspoon salt
1/2 cup sugar
2 tablespoons baking cocoa
3 tablespoons butter
1 large egg (lightly beaten)
1/3 cup milk
1 teaspoon vanilla extract

Directions

For the sauce: combine brown sugar, cocoa, cornstarch, and salt in a large heavy pot. Stir in water. Cook, stirring constantly, until mixture begins to boil and slightly thicken. Add butter, mix well. Remove sauce from heat.

For the dumplings: sift together flour, baking powder, salt, sugar, and cocoa. Cut in butter until mixture resembles a fine meal. Combine the egg, milk, and vanilla. Blend gradually into flour mixture.

Return pot to heat. Bring the chocolate sauce to a boil. Drop dumplings by tablespoons into hot sauce. Reduce heat to low. Cover and simmer until set, about 20 minutes. Serve warm with whipped cream or ice cream.

Norma, Ma Pearl, and Lou

These Dumplings were one of Norma's favorites. Lou would sometimes make them for Norma for her birthday.

Spoiled Grand Baby Soup

Ingredients

1 - blue-eyed, blonde-haired boy
1 - Heaven sent Nana
1 - kitchen that isn't afraid of messes
1 - heaping cup of love
1 - tablespoon of laughter

Directions

Mix the blue-eyed boy and the Heaven-sent Nana together and let them keep company for about an hour, stirring constantly. Then put them both into a messy kitchen, sprinkle around some wooden spoons, measuring cups and a pot or two. Don't worry about adding the love, it came naturally with these two. Let them simmer in the heat until they are bubbling with laughter. Enjoy with a peanut butter sandwich.

Nana and Chapel

Nana and Ashleigh

Ashleigh, Chapel, Christian

Nana and Chapel

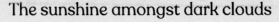

Chloue Rayanne Beysher

The sunshine amongst dark clouds

When I tell the story of my daughter-to-be, I always start with "Let me tell you about my Jesus". If you know me, you know that me and my Nana were always tight, some might even say "attached at the hip". She was truly my best friend. When my Nana first got sick with the dreaded "C" word, it was my prayer that she would one day know my children. At the time, my husband and I knew we weren't yet ready to have children, but it scared me that she might never know her grandchild through me. In December of 2022, my husband and I decided we were ready to start the journey towards parenthood. We know so many that struggle to conceive and figured it would be a couple of years before we would be blessed with children.

A few days after Christmas, I had a dream of my Uncle Patrick, who passed away in 2021 due to a rare form of liver cancer. In my dream, he didn't say a word...he just gave me the biggest smile and hug. I told my family about the dream and found it odd. I knew it had to have a meaning but I just didn't know what and then I quickly forgot about it. About a month later, my cousin Ashleigh messaged me and said "I dreamed you were pregnant". I had no symptoms whatsoever, but decided to take a test to show everyone I was in fact, not. Surprise! The test was positive! I couldn't believe it, but in that moment God reminded me of a promise he had made to me that my Nana would know one of my children this side of Heaven.

My Nana was very sick at that time, with them only giving her months to live. I knew my Nana was one of the first people I had to tell. The joy on her face when I told her I was pregnant was beyond comparison. She was so weak, barely eating, and mainly confined to the bed, but her eyes welled up in joy when I told her the news. A few weeks later I had an appointment where I received my first ultrasound. That evening I immediately drove to Burnsville to show my Nana and she told me "You take care of that little girl". This was months before an anatomy scan would tell me the gender of my baby, but I believe she received a special message from the Heavenly Father.

continued....Chloue Rayanne Beysher
The sunshine amongst dark clouds

My Nana passed away in March and although she didn't meet Chloue this side of Heaven, I believe babies' souls are so pure, that is where they live until we are blessed with them here on Earth, so I believe she met her before the rest of us will in October!

Chloue, we can't wait to meet you and we hope you have your Nana's spunk, her joy for life, and her never-wavering faith in Jesus!

Mikayla

Austin, Nana, Mikayla

Chloue's Mommy & Daddy

Chloue's Gender Reveal

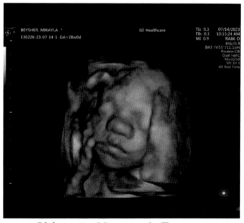

Chloue in Mommy's Tummy

She's Here!

The little girl Nana foretold us about arrived on 9-28-2023 at 7:22 pm

She weighed 7 lbs. 2 oz. and was 19 3/4 inches long. Chloue was named with her Great-Nana's middle name "Lou" in her first name. Rayanne comes from her Great-Papaw Junior Ray and her Uncle Patrick Ray and her Nana Crystal Anne. We are so thankful for this blessing we received at this time in our lives.

Salted Caramel Fudge

This fudge was Nicole's favorite!

Ingredients

3 cups sugar
3/4 cup milk
1-1/2 sticks butter
1 small jar marshmallow cream
1 (12 oz.) package salted caramel chips

Directions

Mix sugar, milk, butter in a pot then bring to a boil. Boil 5 minutes then remove from stove. Stir in salted caramel chips and marshmallow cream. Cool, slice, and serve.

This was the Christmas before I left to go to Oklahoma. She hugged me tight and told me she loves me so much and to make sure to take care of myself and my babies, and that she would pray for us daily. She was my prayer warrior, and I know because of her prayers that my children and I are taken care of just like she wanted.
Nicole

Nicole and her Aunt Lou

Cornbread Dressing
A tradition that Ma Pearl passed down to Lou!

Ingredients
9 cups homemade cornbread (crumbled)
2 cups celery (chopped)
3 cups onions (chopped)
1 teaspoon sage
2-1/2 tablespoons poultry seasoning
1 teaspoon salt
1/2 cup butter (melted)
3-4 cups chicken broth
3 eggs (lightly beaten)
1 cup chicken (cooked)

Directions
Place the crumbled cornbread in a large mixing bowl. Add chopped celery, onions, and mix well. Pour the melted butter over the entire mixture. Pour 3 cups of the broth over the mixture then add more as needed until it is has a thick consistency. Add seasonings, mix well and pour into a greased 9x13 pan. Bake covered at 350 degrees for 30 minutes. Remove cover and bake an additional 30 minutes.

Patrick loved this cornbread dressing!

<u>Cornbread Dressing....continued</u>
David's Favorite!

My favorite times and fondest memories always involved getting together as a family during the holidays. Thanksgiving is always the best. The food is amazing and abundant.

Many years ago, I discovered my favorite dish was Ma Pearl's dressing. Perfect in every way, I couldn't help myself to always want to sample it before everyone else...just to make sure it was still as delicious as the year before. When Ma could no longer make it, I was worried it would never be the same. Aunt Lou proved me totally wrong. Her version was also perfect in every way. Ma passed down many wonderful traits...and not just recipes. Aunt Lou embodied them all and especially the love and care behind her wonderful cooking. She was the best and so was her dressing!

David Fender

David, Ethan, Amy, Lauren, Emma   David and his daughter Lauren

Fried Pies

Ingredients

2 cups self-rising flour
1/4 cup lard
3/4 cup buttermilk
Filling:
6 apples, peeled & sliced (Granny Smith are the best)
1 cup sugar
1/2 stick unsalted butter (room temperature)
1/4 cup water
dash of cinnamon
1-1/2 tablespoons water
1 teaspoon cornstarch
vegetable oil for frying

Directions

Start by making your filling. Place apples, sugar, butter, water, and cinnamon in a saucepan. Cook and stir on medium heat til the apples are tender (about 10-15 minutes). Mix 1.5 tablespoons water and cornstarch together in a cup and pour into the simmering apples to thicken. Remove from heat and let cool completely. For the dough: cut the lard into the flour til crumbly. Add buttermilk til dough is thick. Turn the dough out onto a floured surface, knead, then roll out thin. Cut into 6 inch round pieces. Fill the middle with 2 spoonfuls of filling. Fold dough into half moons then seal edges. Fry in 1 inch of hot oil til golden brown (2-3 minutes on each side). Drain on paper towels or wire racks.

This is picture of Lou's fried pies taken by Patrick in 2021.

Fried Pies....continued
Josh's Favorite!

Out of all the memories I have of Aunt Lou, there is one that stands out above all others. Working 12-hour shifts, I had the privilege of being off in the middle of the week. This allowed me time to go over to the house on the river on Little Creek for an occasional work day with Dad, Uncle Ez, Aunt Lou, and Aunt Norma. This particular day, we had some painting and yard work to do. Once we had finished our work, Lou called everyone in for lunch; fried chicken and all the fixins. If that wasn't enough to put you in a food coma, Lou had fixed homemade fried apple pies. These pies were so good that it almost made your tongue slap your brains out. Out of sheer luck, there were a few left so Lou sent some to Paige so she could partake in the goodness. What we would give to have another one of Lou's fried apple pies....or maybe a whole plate of them.

Josh Fender

Josh and Paige's Wedding Day

Josh, Paige, Jackson, Kraggen

Love Thy Neighbor

Ethel Lou was my second Mom. She was always kind, helpful, and gave me great life advice. In my entire life, I never heard her say an unkind word and was the most faithful person to family, community, and church. If more people were like her, the world would be a better place. I miss her and love her and I hope to live in a manner that is worthy of her example.

John Schuler

John Schuler (neighbor & friend)

Patrick, Crystal, John

Paige, John, and Brayden

Lesley's Memory

I have many memories of Lou Lou. One in particular was when Patrick and I were working at Blue Ridge hospital together and our departments were having a meal together that day for lunch. We were to bring something. Well don't think for one second that Lou didn't make sure and send peanut butter fudge! The best part was that she made sure to tell Pat that some of that was for Johnny. She knew how much he loved her peanut butter fudge. When I brought it home to him that evening, he just couldn't believe she had sent word that he better get some of it! He and the kids thought the world of her also. But, the one thing that keeps coming to mind is....I want to be just like her. What an inspiration! Such a classy lady with her clothes and her high heels, but most of all, she loved Jesus with all her heart, mind, and soul. What a legacy she has left behind for us to follow. I love and miss you Lou Lou.

Lesley Silver

Trevor, Savannah, & Hartley Kate

Gabe & Kennedy

Johnny & Lesley

Hartley Kate

Alivia & Evan

Leia's Memory

Leia also loved the sourdough bread!

I can remember standing in Ma Pearl's kitchen one day and Lou Lou was sharing a memory of me when I was a little girl. She said that I loved coffee, but would always ask for "froffee". She was a true hero to many, and a genuine example of a "Proverbs 31" lady.

If I could give any young person advice, it would be to spend time with your grandparents and loved ones as much as you can. Learn how they do things so that someday, you can pass it on to your family. You may find that some of their traits have been instilled in you. Listen to them. They have a lot of knowledge and wisdom. You may hear a funny story or two and share some laughs together!

"Strength and honour are her clothing; and she shall rejoice in time to come." Proverbs 31:25

Leia Webb

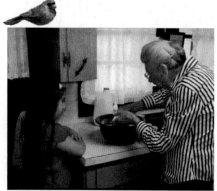

Em learning to make Ma Pearl's biscuits

Lou Lou and
baby Grayson

Leia, Grayson, Lisa, Sandra, Lou, & Sherri
eating at Ma Pearl's table.

Leia, Anthony, & Grayson

"Ethel Lou makes the best peanut
butter fudge and pumpkin roll!"

Anthony Webb

"Lou Lou gave me dollars!"

Grayson Webb

Howard's Batter Bread
"This is like a big biscuit"

Ingredients

1 cup flour
1/3 cup lard
3/4 cup buttermilk

Directions

Preheat oven to 450 degrees. Place lard in an 8" pan and put it in the preheated oven until melted. Pour the melted lard into the flour and buttermilk. Mix well. Pour mixture back into the 8" pan. Bake on 450 degrees for 20 minutes

Ma Pearl & Pa Howard

Nana had this recipe in her collection. She told Crystal that Pa Howard used to make this for the family when Ma Pearl was sick.

<u>Howard's Batter Bread....continued</u>

There are so many times I would call Lou and say "how do I make this", or "how much of this do I put into that", and she always had the time to tell me. She never thought it was crazy that I was in my 30's, 40's, and even my 50's, and still asking questions. She took the time and told me. She taught me to make communion bread for church and that was one of the greatest honors I have ever had.

We were at Lou's one night and out of nowhere, she sat this plate down of the most beautiful, amazing-looking plate of bread I had ever seen. It looked like one huge biscuit and then I tasted it. I couldn't even speak because it was so good. I asked "what is this", and Lou said "it's batter bread, have you never had it?" I was speechless and that is not me. She told me how to make it and now it's a staple around my house. I told my son and daughter and I hope one day they tell their children about their Aunt Lou and the amazing batter bread.

Tina

Crystal, Lou, and Tina

Mickey, Tina, Logan, Bailey

Pinto Beans

Ingredients

1 pound dry pinto beans
2 quarts of water (more when needed)
2 oz. salt pork
1 teaspoon salt

Directions

Soak and wash the beans, discarding any that float or don't look good. Put on to boil in about 2 quarts of water. Add 1-2 ounces of salt pork. Boil on high for about 30 minutes. Cut. down to medium heat and cover then boil for at least another hour. Do not salt until about 15 minutes before serving because salt will prevent the beans from softening while cooking. Add a little water from time to time if beans boil down too much and begin to become too dry. Serve with hot pepper relish.

Be strong and of a good courage; be not afraid, neither be thou dismayed: for the Lord thy God is with thee whithersoever thou goest.
Joshua 1:9

Pinto Beans....continued

Mickey and the "soup beans" story

Growing up at our house, it was a common thing when we went to bed, we would say to each other "night, night, love you", and Daddy would say "soup beans". A lot of people didn't understand how it all went together, but it was just Daddy cutting up. So, Mickey was there one night and we went through our nightly ritual as normal, but when Daddy said "soup beans", Mickey piped up and said "cornbread, buttermilk, and onions".

Crystal

Mickey and Lou

Logan

Mick and Tina

Baleigh

Old Timey Fruitcake

Cake Ingredients
1 cup sugar
1 cup molasses
3/4 cup buttermilk
3/4 cup lard
3 eggs
1 teaspoon ginger
1 teaspoon nutmeg
1 teaspoon cinnamon
6 cups flour

Filling Ingredients
6 apples, peeled & sliced
1 cup sugar
1/2 stick unsalted butter, softened
1/4 cup water
dash of cinnamon
1-1/2 tablespoons water
1 teaspoon cornstarch

Directions

Stir first 8 ingredients in a bowl and mix well. Add to 6 cups flour. Makes a thick dough. Pat out thin in pan. Bake at 400 degrees for 25-30 minutes. Cut into 5-6 cake layers. Make the filling by cooking the first 6 ingredients in a saucepan 10-15 minutes. Stir 1.5 tablespoons water and cornstarch in a cup then pour into apple mixture and stir until thickened, cool completely then spread between layers, then on top and sides.

Nana cutting a piece of her Old-Timey Fruitcake!

Fried Chicken

Nana had a special touch for making fried chicken!

Ingredients

Chicken
Salt & Pepper
Flour
Lard

Directions

Some people argue whether KFC or Chick-fil-a has the best fried chicken, but in our families' opinion...nothing beats fried chicken from Nana's kitchen. What's the secret? Salt and pepper the chicken, then roll it in flour. Fry it in an iron skillet with melted lard. The best part is that it was seasoned with love!

Mikayla

Nana and Mikayla

Alden and Norma

This fried chicken was one of Alden's favorites and Mikayla loved it too!

Higgins Free Will Baptist Church

A small white country church sitting about 1/4 mile off of 19W on Hog Branch in Yancey county was the church that Junior and Ethel Bradford decided to call home. It might have held 100 comfortably and even had outhouses when they first started attending. There was a lot of blood-related family that attended, but in the earlier years, everyone felt like family. There was several different pastors I remember when I was growing up, including Cecil Higgins, Howard Whitson and wife June, Alfred Harris and wife Mildred, Roger Byrd and wife Brenda, Billy Styles and wife Gayle, Keith Miller and wife Tammy, and Adam Bradford and wife Sarah. Daddy (JR) was a deacon for many years. I took piano lessons to be able to play for the church after a pastor left whose wife was our church piano player. Keith Miller was the pastor for over 20 years to Mom. Then when Mom became more sick, her pastor was Adam Bradford, who is also Daddy's 2nd cousin. Daddy would've been so proud to see him pastoring the church that meant so much to us.

A new church was built and Keith got to be the first pastor at the new church. The new church is where Adam is currently the pastor. It is beautiful being black and white brick outside and purple inside with a lot of wood accents and carvings. It would probably hold 500 people. It definitely is a beautiful church, but nothing will ever compare to the feel of the little white country church years ago.

This is preacher Keith Miller and his wife Tammy. Keith was Nana's pastor at Higgins Freewill Baptist Church for over 20 years.

This is preacher Adam Bradford with his wife Sarah and daugher Lydia. Adam was Nana's pastor when she went home to be with the Lord. Adam is also Nana's 2nd cousin by marriage.

Biscuits

Nana was one of the best biscuit-makers on Earth!

Ingredients

2 cups self-rising flour
1/4 cup shortening
3/4 cup buttermilk

Directions

Place flour in a large bowl. Work in your shortening. Add buttermilk until flour until moistened. Turn dough onto lightly floured surface. Knead gently 5-6 times until smooth. Pinch off the dough and shape it into a biscuit. Put a dab of butter on the top of each biscuit. Bake 8-10 minutes or until golden brown in a preheated 475 degree oven. Remove from oven when done. Makes about 12 biscuits.

On the left: Jennifer & Tyler

On the right: Jennifer with her brother Curtis

If you ever left Nana's house hungry, that was on you! Seems like you could smell her cooking from a mile away. What a legacy she left, what a woman she was. We love you Nana!
Jennifer

The Biscuit Story....
Crystal's memory

As I was growing up, I only had a brother and our boy cousins or his friends around most of the time. They would not always allow me to tag along. I had cousins that lived nearby, and sometimes my friends came over, but not a lot. However, for the most part, I was either outside under Dad's feet or inside helping Mom. We would clean which was not much fun or cook which I thoroughly enjoyed. A lot of the time, Mom would get the meat going and I would do the vegetables while she made biscuits. That was one thing I didn't make very much. I could do almost everything else though. One day while in conversation, I asked Mom why she hadn't taught me to make biscuits. She said "I will just make the biscuits and you can do the other stuff". Patrick had to pipe in and say "yeah Mom, teach Crick and maybe hers won't be little, hard, burnt, and brown". Oh no, he had done it now! Daddy and Patrick liked their biscuits big, thick, and barely brown...more like my Nanny Nell's (Dad's Mom), but Mom and I liked ours thin and brown...more like Ma Pearl's (Mom's Mom). So, she decided to tell me and show me a little bit about biscuit-making. She of course, like most women at that time, had her "biscuit-making bowl" with flour already in it. Here are the directions I got: make a well in your flour, put in a hen egg hand full of lard and pour enough buttermilk in to make them the right consistency to be able to pat out and pinch off. What? No wonder she hadn't ever tried to teach me to make biscuits. Who could understand that? Then she said before you put them in the oven, put a dab of butter on the top of each biscuit. That was the only part that made sense to me.

Crystal (Crick)

Mikayla, Jennifer, & Nana.
Jennifer loved Nana's
biscuits!

Chocolate Fudge
Another one of Lou's famous fudge recipes!

Ingredients

3 cups sugar
3/4 cup milk
1-1/2 sticks butter
1 small jar marshmallow cream
1 (12 oz) package chocolate chips

Directions

Mix sugar, milk, butter in a pot then bring to a boil. Boil 5 minutes then remove from stove. Stir in chocolate chips and marshmallow cream. Cool, slice, and serve.

David & Jada
Gianna, Joslyn, Liam, Jack, Luke, & Wyatt

Lou with Joslyn & Gianna

Tangy Barbecue Sandwiches

Ingredients

3 cups chopped celery
1 cup chopped onion
1 cup ketchup
1 cup barbecue sauce
1 cup water
2 tablespoons vinegar
2 tablespoons Worcestershire sauce
2 tablespoons brown sugar
1 teaspoon chili powder
1 teaspoon salt
1/2 teaspoon pepper
1/2 teaspoon garlic powder
1 boneless chuck roast (3-4 lbs. trimmed)
14-18 hamburger buns

Directions

In a slow cooker, combine the first 12 ingredients and mix well. Add roast. Cover and cook on high for 6-7 hours or until tender. Remove roast and let it cool. Shred meat and return to sauce. Heat through. Use a slotted spoon to serve on buns.

Nana, Hope, Damon,
Glendon, & Darius

Norma's Velvet Pound Cake

This cake was another one of Lou's favorites!

Ingredients

3 cups sugar
1-1/2 cups Crisco
1/4 teaspoon salt
2 teaspoons vanilla
1 cup sweet milk
3 cups plain flour
7 eggs

Directions

Preheat oven to 325 degrees. Sift flour 3 times. Mix together sugar, Crisco, salt, and vanilla. Add eggs one at a time, beating after each one. Add milk and flour, alternating between each addition. This will be stiff. Beat well. Grease and flour a tube pan. Pour batter into pan. Bake for 1 hour and 45 minutes. When done, go around inside of pan with a knife. Turn out onto a wire cake cooler.

Crystal and Mike's wedding on the beach!

Newlyweds!

Turtle Cake

Ingredients

1 box Duncan Hines Swiss chocolate or German chocolate cake mix
3 eggs
1/2 cup vegetable oil
1 cup water
1 (14 oz) bag Kraft caramel candies
1/2 stick margarine or butter
1/2 cup milk
1 bag milk chocolate chips
1-1/2 cups chopped pecans

Directions

Preheat oven to 350 degrees. Make cake as directed on the box. Pour
half of the batter into a 9"x13" or 10"x13" cake pan. Bake for 15 minutes,
then remove from oven. In a saucepan, add the caramels, margarine,
and milk. Cook on low until caramels are melted. Pour half of the
caramel mixture over the cooked cake layer. Sprinkle half of the
chocolate chips and chopped pecans all over the caramel layer. Pour
other half of cake batter over the top. Bake for 20 minutes. Remove
from oven then pour other half of the caramel over the finished cake.
Top with other half of the chocolate chips and chopped pecans. Enjoy!

Grandpa Joe Bradford
(Lou's father-in-law)

Granny Nell's Dressing
submitted by her daughter Judy

Ingredients

1 large package Pepperidge Farm stuffing
(2) cans cream of chicken soup
1 medium onion, chopped
3-4 stalks celery, chopped
1 can chicken broth
1/2 cake cornbread
2 tablespoons poultry seasoning

Directions

Preheat oven to 350 degrees. Cook chopped onion and celery on stove until soft. Mix in 2 cans cream of chicken and 2 tablespoons poultry seasoning. Add cornbread and Pepperidge Farm stuffing. Use chicken broth to make it as wet as you desire then bake.

Nanny Nell and Pa Joe

Junior Ray (JR) with his Dad, Pa Joe

Crock Pot Apple Butter

Ingredients

8 cups apples
8 cups sugar
1 box strawberry jello

Directions

Add all three ingredients to a crock pot. Cook for 8 hours. If not thick enough, cook longer.

Chapel playing the piano with his Aunt "Sissy"

Ezra and his Mama " Ma Pearl"

Banana Nut Cupcakes

Ingredients

1/3 cup butter-flavored shortening
2/3 cup sugar
1 cup mashed, ripe bananas (about 3 bananas)
2 eggs
2 tablespoons milk
1 tablespoon vanilla
1-1/3 cups all purpose flour
2 teaspoons baking powder
1/2 teaspoon baking soda
1/4 teaspoon salt
1/4 cup chopped nuts

Directions

In a mixing bowl, cream shortening and sugar. Beat in bananas, eggs, milk, and vanilla. Combine the flour, baking powder, baking soda, and salt. Gradually add flour mixture to the creamed mixture until combined. Stir in nuts. Fill paper-lined muffin cups two-thirds full. Bake at 350 degrees for 18-20 minutes or until a toothpick comes out clean. Cool for 5 minutes then remove from pan and cool on wire racks.

Levi Bradford

Patrick & April Bradford

Smash Cake

Ingredients

1 box yellow cake mix
1 stick butter (melted)
3 eggs
1 box powdered sugar
1 (8 oz) cream cheese
1 teaspoon vanilla

Directions

Preheat oven to 325 degrees. Mix cake mix, 1 egg, and one stick of melted butter with an electric mixer until well combined. Grease a 9 x 13 baking pan. Spread the mixture into the bottom of the pan.

In a large bowl, beat the cream cheese until smooth. Add remaining 2 eggs, vanilla, and powdered sugar. Mix well and pour over the bottom layer. Bake on 325 degrees for 35-40 minutes.

Make sure not to over-bake. The center should be a little gooey.

Brandon & Patrick

Patrick with his Grandson Chapel

Pretty Pickles

Ingredients

12 green tomatoes
12 onions chopped
6 banana peppers
6 red sweet peppers
5 cucumbers cut into circles (peeled and seeded)
1 small head cauliflower
1 cup salt
2 cups vinegar
3 cups sugar
1 cup water
1-1/2 teaspoons turmeric

Directions

Mix first 6 ingredients together then cover with 1 cup of salt. Let stand for 2 hours then drain. In a saucepan, boil the vinegar, sugar, water, and turmeric. Pour over vegetables. Bring to a boil. Place jars and lids in a large pot of very hot water. Pour mixture into hot jars and top with a hot lid so they will seal.

Lou and Ma Pearl used to make these "pretty pickles" at the end of garden season so they wouldn't waste any vegetables.

A memory from Lou's Niece Alicia

First of all, I want to say my sweet Aunt Ethel was one of the sweetest, more caring ladies I had the pleasure of meeting. She was the example of the Christian I desire to be. You could tell by her actions just how much she loved the Lord.

We were both diagnosed with cancer and it's such a horrible disease. I first got diagnosed back in 2008 during my senior year of high school. It was hard being a senior and dealing with that. But, I overcame it with radiation and chemo. I ended up being cancer free for about 8 years or a little longer, in which time, I was able to have a daughter. Then a few years ago, I got diagnosed with colon cancer. It led to me having a colostomy bag as well as a hysterectomy. Aunt Ethel was always rooting me on and telling me how we couldn't quit fighting. I promised her to keep fighting and I have been. Since I had made that promise, all my scans have came back stable with no new growth or spreading! Thank the good Lord above. And with that news, I am currently on a 10 week break from chemo. I miss Aunt Ethel so much, but I am so glad she is healed and with our Lord and Savior watching over each of us. She will always have a special place in my heart, until we meet again. I love you sweet lady!

Alicia

Alicia and daughter Rae

Alicia enjoying Christmas with
her Great-Aunt Ethel Lou

Easy S'more Layer Cake

Ingredients

1 box devil's food cake mix
1 (7 oz) jar marshmallow creme
1/2 cup softened butter
1 (8 oz) container whipped topping thawed
Garnish: crushed graham crackers

Directions

Preheat oven to 350 degrees. Spray 2 (8-inch) round cake pans with cooking spray, then dust with flour. In a large mixing bowl, prepare cake mix according to package. Spoon batter into prepared pans and bake for 25 minutes or until a toothpick comes out clean. Cool for 10 minutes. Remove from pans and cool completely on wire racks. Using a serrated knife, cut each layer in half horizontally. In a medium bowl, beat marshmallow creme and butter until smooth. Add whipped topping and beat until slightly thickened. On a serving platter, place one cake layer cut side down. Spread 1/4 of the marshmallow creme mixture over the top of the layer. Repeat this process with the other three layers. Top with crushed graham crackers.

Nell Bradford
(Lou's mother-in-law)

Barbecued Meatballs

Telina loved Lou's Meatballs!

Meatball Ingredients

1 egg (lightly beaten)
1 can (5 oz.) evaporated milk
1 cup quick-cooking oats
1/2 cup finely chopped onion
1 teaspoon salt
1 teaspoon chili powder
1/4 teaspoon garlic powder
1/4 teaspoon pepper
1-1/2 pounds ground beef

Sauce Ingredients

1 cup ketchup
3/4 cup packed brown sugar
1/4 cup chopped onion
1/2 teaspoon liquid smoke
* (the liquid smoke is optional)
1/4 teaspoon garlic powder

Note: Nana also used this sauce for her meatloaf and ribs.

Directions

In a bowl, combine the first eight ingredients. Crumble beef over mixture and mix well. Shape into 1-inch balls then place into a greased 9 x 13 baking dish. Bake at 350 degrees for 18-20 minutes or until no longer pink. Mix all the sauce ingredients together in a sauce pan. Cook on low heat until hot. Pour over cooked meatballs then place back in the oven for 12-15 minutes.

On the left:
Telina and Lou

On the right:
Ross, Telina, Victoria, and Brennan

Communion and Unleavened Bread

Another important recipe for Nana was communion bread. Just two simple ingredients, water and plain flour, represented so much. It was significant that the flour used to make communion bread was plain flour, because communion bread is supposed to be "unleavened" or have no agent in it that would cause it to rise. I think the bread being unleavened is important because Jesus made himself lowly so that we could be saved and it is a reminder for us to stay humble. Nana was like unleavened bread. To the outside world, she may look simple, but there is no communion without communion bread and her family's lives would be incomplete without her. It was her job to make the communion bread for the service designated to remember the sacrifice that Jesus made on the cross. I often wonder what other ingredients she added that made the communion bread so special. Ingredients like love, prayer, and devotion. I often wonder if some of her tears fell into the bread as she cried out to God to bless the service as she cut the bread into tiny squares so that each person could take part. I believe those tears were filled with the Holy Spirit, and I wonder if she went through each pew, praying for each person that would take part in the communion service. While Nana got the communion bread together, her best friend Anise provided the grape juice. The grape juice was not just simple grape juice bought from the store, but homemade grape juice, made from grapes that grew on vines on the side of the barn by Anise's house. This was usually canned the old-fashioned way, such as on a wood stove or even an outside fire. The practice of communion comes from the scripture in Luke chapter 22, verses 1-20. Jesus asked the disciples to participate in communion "in remembrance of me". The bread represents Jesus' body that he sacrificed for us and the grape juice, the blood that he shed. Not only did they make the communion bread and grape juice, but Nana and Anise took special care to set up the communion table, carefully placing the little squares of bread on trays and pouring tiny glasses of grape juice, careful not to spill a drop. There was a somber feeling as soon as you walked in the door of the church as you watched these ladies prepare the table. Communion was to be taken seriously. Nana and Anise also filled the basins that would be used for the foot washing part of the service. Another part of communion was the foot washing service which comes from John chapter 13, verses 5-10. Jesus, Lord of the universe, humbled himself and washed the disciples feet. At the communion service, after the taking of the bread and grape juice, the men would depart into one of the classrooms and the women stayed in the sanctuary and we would all humble ourselves and wash each other's feet. It was often quiet during this time besides whispered prayers as women prayed over each other as they washed each other's feet. After the service was over, the children of the church would gather around the communion table, begging for the leftover communion bread and the extra grape juice, which Anise and Nana were happy to give with the reminder to the children that they never forget the significance of this service.

Mikayla

This is what the finished bread looks like when prepared for communion.

Ingredients

1 cup all-purpose flour
1/3 cup vegetable oil
1/8 teaspoon salt
1/3 cup water

Directions

Preheat oven to 425 degrees. Line a baking sheet with parchment paper. Mix flour, vegetable oil, and salt together in a bowl. Add water and mix until dough is soft. Form into several balls. Press into disks onto prepared baking sheet with your hands. Bake in preheated oven until bread is cooked (8-10 minutes).

New York's Finest Cheesecake

Crust Ingredients

1-1/2 cups graham cracker crumbs
1/4 sugar
1/4 cup unsalted butter, melted

Topping Ingredients

1 container (16 oz) sour cream
1/4 cup sugar
1 teaspoon vanilla

Cheesecake Ingredients

3 packages (8 oz each) cream cheese
1-1/4 cups sugar
4 eggs
2 teaspoons vanilla
2 teaspoons fresh lemon juice

Directions

Preheat oven to 350 degrees. Prepare crust: combine crumbs, sugar, and butter in a bowl. Scrape into a 9-inch springform pan. Press evenly over bottom and 1 inch up the sides. Prepare cheesecake: beat cream cheese and sugar at medium speed in a large bowl until blended. Beat in eggs, vanilla, and lemon juice until blended. Pour into prepared pan. Bake in 350 degree oven for 50 minutes or until puffed and golden. Transfer to a wire rack and let stand for 15 minutes. Increase oven to 450 degrees. Prepare topping: Stir together sour cream, sugar and vanilla until well blended. Spoon over top of cheesecake, spreading evenly. Bake 10 minutes just until the topping is set. Transfer cheesecake to rack to cool completely. Refrigerate overnight.

__New York's Finest Cheesecake continued....__

This cheesecake was Jake's favorite!

Becky's son Jake

Becky's daughter Abby Grace
with Nana

Becky's son Zach and
his wife Lexie

Molasses Popcorn Balls

Ingredients

1 cup molasses
1 cup corn syrup
1 teaspoon vinegar
3 tablespoons butter
1/2 teaspoon salt
3 quarts popped corn

Directions

Mix molasses, syrup, and vinegar in a large saucepan and cook til molasses dropped in cold water becomes brittle. Add remaining ingredients. Form into balls. Cool and enjoy!

Nana and Cousin Brandon

Annual Christmas Gathering

24 Hour Slaw

Ingredients

1 large head of cabbage
3/4 cup sugar
1 onion
1 teaspoon sugar for sauce
1 teaspoon celery seed
1 cup vinegar
3/4 cup Wesson oil

Directions

Grate cabbage then mix with sugar. Cut the onion into rings and add to the cabbage mixture. Let this mixture stand while preparing the sauce. For the sauce: add 1 teaspoon sugar, celery seed, vinegar, and Wesson oil to a saucepan. Bring to a boil, then pour over cabbage. Chill in fridge overnight.

Nana's Aunt Caroline and
cousins Angie and Kelly

Nana and her cousin Jeff

Ma Pearl with her nephew Craig

Lemon Lush

Ingredients

For the Crust
1 cup self-rising flour
1 stick melted butter
1 cup chopped nuts

2nd Layer
2 packages lemon instant pudding mix
2 cups cold milk
optional: shredded coconut for the top

1st Layer
1 (8 oz) block cream cheese
2 tablespoons milk
1 (8 oz) cool whip
1 cup powdered sugar

Note: this recipe uses (3.4 oz) boxes of pudding mix. If you buy (5.9 oz) boxes, increase the cold milk to 3 cups.

Directions

For the Crust:
Mix all crust ingredients together and spread into a 9 x 13 pan. Bake on 350 degrees for 15-20 minutes. Let cool completely.

For Layer #1:
Mix all ingredients together and spread half of the mixture over the cooled crust.

For Layer #2:
Blend pudding mix with cold milk until thick. Pour over Layer #1.

For Layer #3:
Pour the remaining cream mixture (from layer #1) over the pudding mixture (layer #2). If this is too thick, add a little milk and beat.

Sprinkle coconut over the top if you wish

Butterscotch Delight

Ingredients

2 cups plain flour
2 sticks melted butter
1 cup chopped pecans
2 (8 oz) containers cool whip
8 oz cream cheese
1 1/2 cups powdered sugar
2 boxes instant butterscotch pudding
3 cups milk
more chopped pecans to sprinkle on top

Directions

Preheat oven to 375 degrees. Mix together the first 3 ingredients. Press into a 9x13 pan and bake for 15-20 minutes then cool completely. Mix together 1 container of cool whip, cream cheese, and powdered sugar. Spread over the cooled crust. Mix both boxes of pudding mix with 3 cups of milk. Spread over cream cheese layer. Top with the remaining container of cool whip. Sprinkle with remaining chopped nuts. Chill 2-3 hours.

Randall and Melanie Fender

Lou's brother Ezra and
her granddaughter Ashleigh

Chicken Casserole

Ingredients

4 large chicken breasts (cooked & shredded)
1 can cream of mushroom soup
1 can cream of chicken soup
2 cans chicken broth
1 stick melted butter
1 bag Pepperidge Farm cornbread dressing
Optional: 1 chopped onion

Directions

Preheat oven to 350 degrees. Mix melted butter with cornbread dressing. Dilute each can of soup with 1 can of broth. Put a layer of dressing, then a layer of chicken, then a layer of soup. Repeat layers one more time. Save enough dressing to sprinkle over the top. Bake in a 350 degree oven for 30 minutes. Optional: add chopped onion if desired.

Morgan, Alivia, Emery, & Baleigh

Devin & Baleigh

Goulash

Ingredients

2 cups cooked macaroni
1 pint tomatoes
1 lb. ground beef

Directions

Cook macaroni. Brown beef. Combine. Add tomatoes and let simmer for 5 minutes.

Ethan Wilson

Amy Wilson

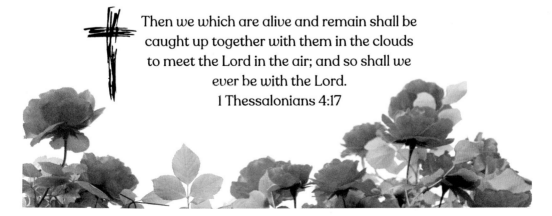

Then we which are alive and remain shall be caught up together with them in the clouds to meet the Lord in the air; and so shall we ever be with the Lord.
1 Thessalonians 4:17

Granny's Sugar Cookies

Ingredients

1/2 cup butter
1 cup sugar
1 egg
1/2 teaspoon salt
2 teaspoons baking powder
2 cups flour (sifted)
1/2 teaspoon vanilla

Directions

Preheat oven to 400 degrees. Cream together the butter and sugar. Add in the egg and mix well. In a separate bowl, sift together the salt, baking powder, and flour. Add the flour mixture to the butter mixture and mix until fully combined. Add in the vanilla and mix well. Spread the dough out and cut with cookie cutters. Place cookies onto a greased baking sheet and bake at 400 degrees for 8-10 minutes.

Steve & Debbie Grindstaff   RC Bryant   Mike & Sandy Holt

Some very special friends of our family

South-of-the-Border Chili

Ingredients

1 lb. ground beef
2 cans tomato soup
3 cups cooked macaroni
3 tablespoons chili powder
1/2 teaspoon salt
1 cup chopped onion
2 cans beans (kidney, pinto, or chili)
1/2 cup water
2 teaspoons vinegar
dash of pepper

Directions

In a large saucepan, brown beef and cook until tender. Add remaining ingredients, stir, and simmer for 30 minutes, stirring occasionally.

Nana and her nephew Sam

Patrick, Nana, & Tim

Crystal's Lasagna

This was Lou's favorite dish that Crystal made!

Ingredients

1 lb. ground beef
3/4 cup chopped onion
2 tablespoons oil
1 can stewed tomatoes
2 cans tomato paste
2 cups water
1 tablespoon parsley
1/2 cup parmesan cheese
2 teaspoons salt
1 tablespoon sugar
1 teaspoon garlic powder
1/2 teaspoon oregano
1/2 teaspoon pepper
1 lb. ricotta cheese
8 oz. mozzarella cheese
9 lasagna noodles

Directions

In a large skillet, brown beef and onions in oil. Add stewed tomatoes, tomato paste, water, parsley, salt, sugar, garlic powder, oregano, and pepper. Let simmer 30 minutes. Cook noodles 10 minutes (9 noodles-add 1/2 tsp. salt & 1 tbsp. oil in water). In a baking dish, spread a layer of sauce in bottom of pan, then noodles, then ricotta cheese, then sauce, then noodles, then mozzarella cheese, then sauce, then noodles, then parmesan cheese. Bake at 350 degrees for 30 minutes.

Peanut Butter No Bake Cookies

Ingredients

1/2 cup peanut butter
1/2 cup butter
2 cups granulated sugar
1/2 cup cold milk
3-1/2 cups quick cooking oats
1 tablespoon vanilla extract

Directions

Add the butter, sugar, and milk to a heavy bottomed pot. Bring to a rolling boil and boil for 1 minute while stirring. Take the pot off the heat and mix in the peanut butter, vanilla, and oats. Use a spatula to scoop and drop the cookie mixture onto a piece of parchment paper to cool.

The gatherings at Ma and Pa's house are always a blast and even though the house is always crowded....it is full of love. The Christmas story is read from the Bible every Christmas Eve with the entire family gathered around.

Stormy's Oatmeal Candy

Ingredients

2 cups sugar
2 heaping tablespoons cocoa
2/3 cup cream or milk
1/2 stick butter sliced into pats
1/2 to 1/3 cup peanut butter
1 tablespoon vanilla
2 cups instant oats

Nana and Norma with their neighbor
and close friend Stormy

Directions

Blend sugar and cocoa together. Stand child on a chair beside you. Use a spoon to make a funny face with big eyes and mouth. Let the child helping you pour the cream into the eyes and mouth trying not to go over the edges. While child is pouring cream, you make a funny voice. Once trenches for face is filled, let child blend it all together while you tell them to mash it all up! Please note: this step is crucial to the outcome of the candy. All my nieces and nephews can attest to this!

Put pot on the stove on medium heat. Stir in butter until melted, then add peanut butter. Once peanut butter is melted, add vanilla. Bring to a rolling boil. Once boiling, set timer for 4 minutes and continue stirring. After 4 minutes, add oats. Continue cooking and stirring for 1 minute so the oats have time to cook. Spoon onto parchment paper. Let cool for 3 minutes.

If you don't get to do the step with the child above, it may not set right. In that case, grab a tablespoon and scoop it up because it's still tasty!

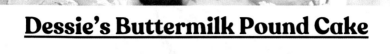

Dessie's Buttermilk Pound Cake

Ingredients

1 cup plain flour (sifted)
2 cups sugar
1 cup Crisco oil
1/2 teaspoon baking soda
1/4 teaspoon salt
1 cup buttermilk
3 eggs
1 teaspoon lemon flavoring
1 teaspoon orange flavoring

Directions

Mix all ingredients. Pour into a tube pan that is well greased. Bake at 275-300 degrees for 90 minutes.

This is Dessie Honeycutt,
a neighbor and friend to Nana

Chocolate Roulade

This can be made two different ways.

Roulade Ingredients

1/4 cup cocoa plus 3 tablespoons divided
5 eggs
3/4 cup sugar
3/4 cup all purpose flour
1 teaspoon vanilla
1 teaspoon baking powder
1/4 teaspoon salt

Peanut Butter Filling

1 cup powdered sugar
1 (8 oz) cream cheese
1 cup sour cream
1 cup peanut butter

Raspberry Filling

1/2 cup powdered sugar
1 (8 oz) cream cheese
1 cup raspberry jam

Directions

Preheat oven to 375 degrees. Spray a 15x10 inch jelly roll pan with cooking spray, line with wax paper, then spray again. Sprinkle 1 tablespoon cocoa powder into bottom of pan. Separate egg yolks from egg whites. In a medium bowl, beat egg yolks until thick and pale. Gradually add 1/2 cup sugar, 1/4 cup cocoa, flour, and vanilla. Beat until smooth. In a separate bowl, beat egg whites until foamy. Gradually add 1/4 cup sugar and beat until stiff. Fold into cocoa mixture. Pour into pan and bake 10-11 minutes. Sift 2 tablespoons cocoa onto paper towels. Pour the jelly roll onto paper towels to cool. Spread the filling of your choice all over the jelly roll. Roll up carefully, slice, and serve.

The Annual Egg Toss Game
Jackson's Story

The egg toss originated (Tina's idea), many moons ago and is always played on Easter. Teams of two toss an egg until the egg breaks. You toss and then take a step back each time after tossing. Now the breaking of the egg could be due to a number of things. One partner might not throw it very far (Tina), one partner might let it slip through their hands and just not catch it, or possibly a partner just beams it in the air and the egg breaks all over them. I've always stuck by a saying when it comes to the egg toss and that is, "Be one with the egg". Gabe and I have lived by that motto especially when it comes to a certain gathering toward the end of March or in early April. That motto has gifted us 7 wins which is quite impressive and hopefully a couple more in the future. A couple of those should have been victories, but sadly were not. Always remember when participating in "The Egg Toss", to live by the quote and you too could become victorious!

Jackson Fender

The Champs
Jackson & Gabe

Crystal and Patrick playing
"The Egg Toss" game

Strawberry Banana Crepes

Crepe Ingredients

1 cup all purpose flour
1 tablespoon sugar
1/2 teaspoon cinnamon
1-1/2 cups milk
2 eggs
1 to 2 tablespoons butter

Filling Ingredients

1 package (8 oz) cream cheese (softened)
8 oz. whipped topping (thawed)
1/2 cup powdered sugar

Topping Ingredients

2 cups sliced fresh strawberries
2 medium firm bananas sliced
1/4 cup sugar, optional

Directions

In a mixing bowl, combine the flour, sugar, cinnamon, milk, and eggs. Mix well. Cover and refrigerate for 1 hour. In an 8-inch, nonstick skillet, melt 1 teaspoon butter. Stir batter and pour about 2 tablespoons into the center of skillet. Lift and tilt pan to evenly coat bottom. Cook until top appears dry. Turn and cook 15-20 seconds longer. Remove to a wire rack. Repeat with remaining batter, adding butter to the skillet as needed. When cool, stack crepes with waxed paper or paper towels in between. In a mixing bowl, combine the filling ingredients. Spread 2 tablespoonfuls on each crepe. Roll up. Combine topping ingredients and spoon over crepes.

Nana, Georgia, and Albert Dean (Eb)

Sausage Balls

Ingredients

1 lb. bulk sausage (mild or hot)
1 (10 oz) package extra sharp cheese
1 teaspoon paprika
3 cups biscuit mix

Directions

Sit sausage and cheese out to room temperature then combine to mix well. Add paprika and biscuit mix to sausage mixture then mix well. Roll into small balls. Bake at 350 degrees for 12-15 minutes. This makes 100 sausage balls. May be baked and frozen for unexpected company.

Barbara and Don Everhart

Don and Patrick

Barbara and Lou

Banana Pudding

Ingredients

10 tablespoons flour
2 cups sugar
4 cups milk
2 tablespoons vanilla
1 stick butter
4 egg yolks
1 box vanilla wafers
7 bananas

Directions

Cook flour, sugar, milk, vanilla, butter, and egg yolks on medium to medium-high heat until thick. In a large, ovenproof bowl, layer: wafers, bananas, and pudding mixture. In a separate bowl, beat egg whites to make a meringue. Place meringue on top then brown in the oven.

Cason, Glendon, Gabby, Damon,
Colson, Devin, and Mandy

Honey Bun Cake

Ingredients

1 box yellow cake mix
3/4 cup oil
1 cup sour cream (8 oz)
4 eggs
3/4 cup brown sugar
3 teaspoons cinnamon
2 cups powdered sugar
1 teaspoon vanilla
8 tablespoons milk

Directions

Mix together cake mix, oil, sour cream, and eggs. In a separate bowl, mix together the brown sugar and cinnamon. Pour half of the batter into a 9"x 13" baking dish. Sprinkle half of brown sugar mixture over cake batter, add remaining half of cake batter and sprinkle the rest of the brown sugar on top. Swirl with a case knife. Preheat oven to 350 degrees and bake for 35-40 minutes. Glaze: mix powdered sugar, vanilla, and milk. Stir until desired thickness. Pour glaze over cooled cake.

Mama and Long-Time Family Friend Theresa Lytle

Larry Fender and Long-Time Family Friend Donnie Lytle

Butterscotch Candy

Ingredients

2 cups brown sugar
1 cup sugar
1 cup milk
1 stick butter
2 (6 oz) bags butterscotch chips
1 jar marshmallow cream

Directions

Mix sugars, butter, and milk in a saucepan. Boil 15 minutes then remove from heat. Stir in butterscotch chips and marshmallow cream. Pour into a buttered dish, cool, slice, and serve!

Granny Edna at Ma Pearl's House.

Edna McFalls
(Sandra Fender's Mother)

Edna always thought the world of Lou. She loved going to the house on the river with Larry and Sandra to spend the day with Lou and the rest of the family.

Cream Cheese Brownies

This recipe belongs to Georgia Bradford.

1st Layer Ingredients

1 box yellow cake mix
1 stick margarine, melted
1 egg

2nd Layer Ingredients

1 (8 oz) cream cheese, softened
1 box (10x) powdered sugar
3 eggs

Directions

Preheat oven to 325 degrees.

For the crust: mix together the cake mix, margarine, and 1 egg until well blended then press into a 9x13 baking dish.

For the 2nd layer: mix cream cheese, powdered sugar, and 3 eggs together until well blended. Pour on top of the first layer. Bake for 55 minutes.

Lou with her brother-in-law, Eb Bradford (Georgia's husband)

Georgia and Lou

Chocolate Peanut Butter Balls

Ingredients

2 sticks melted butter
1 cup graham crackers (crushed)
1 cup chopped pecans
1 can coconut
1 cup peanut butter
1 box powdered sugar
1 teaspoon salt
6 oz. chocolate or butterscotch
1/2 block paraffin wax

Directions

Mix first 7 ingredients together with your hands. Shape into small balls. Melt 6 oz. chocolate or butterscotch and 1/2 block paraffin wax in a double boiler. Dip balls and place on wax paper.

Lou and Amy (David's wife)

Amy, David, Josh, Paige, Mel, Randall

Miniature Cheesecakes

Ingredients

2 cups graham cracker crumbs (more if needed)
3/4 cup sugar plus 2-1/2 teaspoons
2 (8 oz) blocks cream cheese
4 egg yolks & 4 egg whites
3/4 cup sour cream
1 teaspoon vanilla
chopped pecans and fruit topping (optional)

Directions

Cover the bottoms of muffin tins with graham cracker crumbs. Mix together 3/4 cup sugar, 2 blocks cream cheese, and 4 egg yolks. Beat egg whites until stiff then fold into cream cheese mixture. Fill muffin tins full and bake at 350 degrees for 15 minutes. Let cool completely. Heat the oven to 400 degrees. Mix together 3/4 cup sour cream, 2 1/2 teaspoons sugar, and vanilla. Fill center of cakes. Top with pecans and return to oven. Bake for 5 minutes. Top with fruit topping of your choosing.

Mike and Mama at Mayberry

Chicken Pot Pie

Ingredients

4 boneless skinless chicken breasts (cut into cubes)
1 cup coarsely chopped onion
2 tablespoons butter or oil
1 package (.9 oz) chicken gravy mix
1 cup milk
2 cans (15 oz each) mixed vegetables (drained)
1 (9-inch) refrigerated pie crust

Directions

Preheat oven to 425 degrees. Cook chicken and onion in butter in a large skillet over medium-high heat for 5 minutes. Stir in gravy mix and milk. Cook, stirring until thickened. Add vegetables. Spoon into a deep dish pie plate or shallow casserole dish. Top with crust; folding edge under. Bake at 425 degrees for 15 minutes or until crust is golden brown.

Patrick with cousins Tim and Sam

Spaghetti and Meat Sauce

Ingredients

1 lb. ground beef
1 onion (finely chopped)
1 green pepper (chopped)
1 garlic clove (diced)
1 celery stalk (chopped)
1 teaspoon chili powder
1 (6 oz) can tomato paste
1 cup water
1/3 cup ketchup
1 teaspoon salt
1 teaspoon vinegar
1 tablespoon sugar

Directions

Brown beef with onion, pepper, garlic, and celery. Once meat is browned, add all other ingredients. Simmer on low heat for 30 minutes. Pour over cooked spaghetti noodles.

Nana's grandson
Levi

Levi with his
nephew Chapel

April's Shrimp

Nana loved when April made this shrimp!

Ingredients

1 stick butter
1 packet of dry Italian seasoning
Shrimp (ever how much you like)
1 box cooked spaghetti
feta cheese
garlic bread

Directions

Melt 1 stick of butter in an oven dish. Add shrimp. Sprinkle dry Italian seasoning packet over the shrimp. Bake at 350 degrees for 20 minutes until shrimp is pink and done. Pour over the cooked spaghetti noodles. Sprinkle feta cheese over the top. Serve with garlic bread.

Brayden and Nana

Brayden and Nana

Cream Cheese Frosting

Ingredients

1 stick butter
1/4 teaspoon salt
1 block (8 oz) cream cheese
3-1/2 cups powdered sugar
1 teaspoon vanilla

Directions

Beat the butter and salt together until smooth. Add the cream cheese, powdered sugar, and vanilla. Beat until well mixed. Refrigerate until ready to use.

Nana with her friend Maggie

Nana with her friend Vanetta

Punch Bowl Cake

Ingredients

1 box yellow cake mix
2 containers fresh strawberries (sliced)
1 package strawberry glaze
2 boxes vanilla pudding mix
1 container (16 oz) cool whip

Directions

Make cake according to the instructions on the box in two (9-inch) round cake pans. Cool cakes then cut each cake in half lengthwise with a string to make 4 cake layers in total. Make pudding as directed on the boxes. In a separate bowl, stir together the strawberries and glaze. In the bottom of a punchbowl or trifle bowl, place a layer of cake, then top with a layer of strawberry mixture, then a layer of pudding mixture, then a layer of cool whip. Repeat with 3 more layers ending with cool whip on top. Refrigerate until ready to serve.

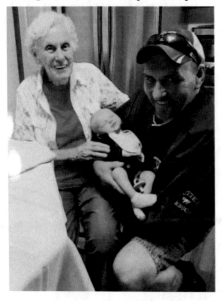

Nana with her cousin Todd,
and baby Chapel

Mexican Cornbread

Ingredients

2 cups cornmeal
1 cup flour
1/2 cup sharp cheddar cheese (grated)
3 jalapeno peppers (diced)
1/2 can creamed corn
1 large onion (diced)
1 cup buttermilk
2 eggs
2/3 cup vegetable oil

Directions

Preheat oven to 375 degrees. Mix all ingredients together. Pour into a 9x13 greased baking dish. Bake for 1 hour.

Ma Pearl's brother Creed

Creed's wife Mamie, and daughter Dana with Lou and Crystal in Tybee Island, GA

Anise's Dill Pickles

Ingredients

1 quart vinegar
4 quarts water
1 cup pickling salt
Alum
Cucumbers
Garlic Cloves
Grape Leaves
Red Pepper Flakes
16-18 pint canning jars

Directions

In the bottom of every jar, put 1/4 teaspoon red pepper flakes, 1 garlic clove, and less than 1/4 teaspoon alum.
Put vinegar, water, and pickling salt in a pot and bring to a rolling boil.
Pack cucumbers into the jars. Pour vinegar mixture over cucumbers until covered. Place a grape leave on top then put the lid on.
Wait 6 weeks before eating. You can half the recipe for a small run.

This is Anise Bailey
(Nana's friend that
gave her this recipe).

<u>Anise's Butter Pecan Cake</u>

<u>Ingredients</u>

1 box butter pecan cake mix
3/4 cup vegetable oil
4 eggs
1 cup water
1/4 cup powdered sugar
1/4 cup chopped pecans
1 can butter pecan frosting

<u>Directions</u>

Preheat oven to 325 degrees. Grease the bottom of a 9"x13" glass or metal baking dish. Sprinkle the powdered sugar and nuts over the bottom of the dish. Mix together the cake mix, oil, eggs, and water until well blended. Pour batter into baking pan and bake for 55 minutes or until a toothpick comes out clean. Spread frosting over the cooled cake.

Levi peacefully resting beside his Nana

Pizza Dough

Ingredients

1 cup lukewarm water
1 teaspoon sugar
1/4 teaspoon salt
2 teaspoons dry yeast
1-1/2 cups flour (sifted)
2 tablespoons melted shortening

Directions

Mix lukewarm water, sugar, and salt in a bowl. Sprinkle yeast over water mixture and let stand for 5 minutes (do not stir). Stir flour into water and yeast mixture. This dough should be stiff enough to form a ball. If it is not, gradually add more flour, a tablespoon at a time, not to exceed 4 tablespoons in all. Add melted shortening and mix. Let dough rise until doubled in size. Spread dough in a greased pizza pan. Cover with meat sauce and grated cheese. Bake on 425 degrees for 15-20 minutes.

Nana with her Granddaughters (Mikayla and Ashleigh)

Mom's Special Chicken Soup

This is the soup that Lou always made at Christmas.

Ingredients

1 broiler-fryer chicken (3.5-4 lbs)
3 quarts water
1 medium onion, quartered
4 celery ribs
2 chicken bouillon cubes
2 parsley sprigs
1 garlic clove
2-1/2 teaspoons salt
1/2 cup thinly sliced carrots
1/2 cup chopped fresh parsley
3 cups cooked rice

Directions

Place chicken and water in a large kettle or dutch oven. Bring to a boil. Reduce heat. Add onion, celery, bouillon, parsley sprigs, garlic, and salt. Cover and simmer until the chicken is tender (about 1 hour). Remove chicken and allow to cool. Strain and reserve broth. Discard the vegetables. Add carrots to broth and simmer until tender (about 15 minutes). Debone the chicken then cut into cubes. Add chicken and chopped parsley to broth, heat through. Ladle into bowls. Add rice to each bowl.

Junior Ray with his sister Judy

<u>Southern Sweet Potato Pie</u>

<u>Ingredients</u>

3 tablespoons all-purpose flour
1-2/3 cups sugar
1 cup mashed sweet potatoes
2 eggs
1/4 cup light corn syrup
1/4 teaspoon ground nutmeg
a pinch of salt
1/2 cup butter or margarine
3/4 cup evaporated milk
1 (9 inch) unbaked pastry shell

<u>Directions</u>

In a large mixing bowl, combine flour and sugar. Add sweet potatoes, eggs, corn syrup, nutmeg, salt, butter, and evaporated milk. Beat well. Pour into pastry shell. Bake at 350 degrees for 55-60 minutes.

Lou and Sherri at the family cemetery on the hill.

Graham Cracker Squares

Ingredients

1/2 stick butter
1 egg (well beaten)
1/2 cup milk
1 cup sugar
1 cup graham cracker crumbs
1 cup chopped pecans
1 cup coconut
1 (8 oz) block cream cheese
1 cup confectioners sugar
1 box graham crackers

Directions

Place butter, egg, milk, and sugar in a saucepan and bring to a boil then remove from heat. Stir in graham cracker crumbs, pecans, and coconut. Mix well. Spread mixture between graham crackers like sandwiches. Beat the cream cheese, powdered sugar, and a splash of milk together until smooth (add more milk if too thick to spread). Spread cream cheese mixture on tops of graham cracker sandwiches like icing.

Levi Bradford & Josh Fender

Larry, Kraggen, & Sandra Fender

Crystal's Bean Salad

This recipe didn't really have a name so Mama named it "Crystal's Bean Salad". Mikayla always called it "Bean Stuff".

Ingredients

1 (15-16 oz) can light red kidney beans (drained)
1 (15-16 oz) can dark red kidney beans (drained)
1 (15-16 oz) can black olives (sliced)
1 (15-16 oz) can whole kernel corn (drained)
1 green pepper (diced)
1 onion (diced)
1 tomato (diced)
1 (16 oz) jar catalina dressing

Directions

Mix all ingredients together well. That's all! It's ready to eat.

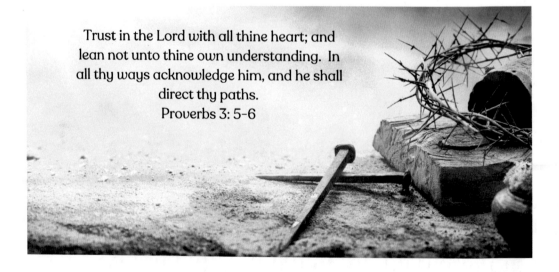

Trust in the Lord with all thine heart; and lean not unto thine own understanding. In all thy ways acknowledge him, and he shall direct thy paths.
Proverbs 3: 5-6

Pumpkin Pie

Ingredients

1 (15 oz) can pumpkin
1 (12 oz) can evaporated milk
2 eggs (beaten)
3/4 cup brown sugar
1/2 teaspoon salt
1/2 teaspoon cinnamon
1/4 teaspoon nutmeg
1 deep dish pie crust

Directions

Preheat oven to 450 degrees. Beat all ingredients together until mixed well. Pour into the pie crust. Bake 20 minutes. Reduce heat to 350 degrees then bake for an additional 35 minutes.

Nana and her sister-in-law Judy

Hominy Salad

Ingredients

1 can white hominy
1/4 cup chopped green pepper
2 tablespoons chopped onion
1/2 cup chopped celery
1/2 cup pickle relish (drained)
1 teaspoon salt
1/4 teaspoon pepper
1/4 teaspoon celery seed
1 cup cubed or grated cheese
1 cup mayonnaise
(add sugar if desired)

Directions

Rinse hominy and drain well. Combine with remaining ingredients and chill well. Serve on lettuce garnished with tomato wedges and more mayonnaise if desired. To make a main dish out of this salad, add a can of drained tuna, or a cup of diced ham. You also can add a few chopped boiled eggs instead.

This is Harold and Linda Webb. Harold was Larry and Norma's pastor at Liberty Freewill Baptist Church for many years. Harold and Linda have always been there for the family including hospital visits and bringing goodies. They are a huge blessing to everyone.

Evergreen Punch

Ingredients

2 packs lime Kool-Aid
1 quart ginger ale
1 large can pineapple juice
2 cups sugar
1 quart hot water
1 quart cold water

Directions

Dissolve sugar in one quart of hot water. Add one quart of cold water. Stir kool aid packs and pineapple juice into the sugar water. Stir in the ginger ale just before serving. Serve over ice.

Norma & Don with their
daughter Jada

Tina's wedding day with
her Daddy Don

Salsa for canning

Ingredients

8 quarts of cut tomatoes
5 garlic cloves (evenly chopped)
8 bell peppers
8 hot peppers
5 onions (chopped)
5 tablespoons cilantro
7 tablespoons basil
5 teaspoons cumin
3 teaspoons chili powder
7 tablespoons salt
3 teaspoons black pepper
9 tablespoons sugar
5 tablespoons vinegar

Directions

Place all ingredients in a large pot and bring to a boil. Simmer for 15 minutes. Taste to adjust seasoning to your liking. Pour into jars. Put lids on jars then place jars into a water bath for 10-15 minutes. Enjoy!

Brandon Fender and his
Fiance Kelsey

Frozen Blueberry Muffins

Ingredients

2 cups all purpose flour
2 teaspoons baking powder
1/4 teaspoon salt
1/2 cup oil or softened margarine
1 cups sugar
2 eggs
1/2 cup milk
1 teaspoon vanilla
1 cup frozen blueberries
For the topping:
2 tablespoons sugar
1/2 teaspoon nutmeg

Directions

Preheat oven to 375 degrees. Combine the flour, baking powder, and salt. In a mixing bowl, cream the butter and sugar together. Add milk, eggs, and vanilla then mix well. Stir this mixture into the dry ingredients just until moistened. Fold in blueberries. Pour into muffin cups. Sprinkle topping over each muffin. Bake at 375 degrees for 20-25 minutes.

This is Pa Howard's niece Doris Bradford and her husband Larry Bradford. Nana and Doris were first cousins and big buddies!

Blooper Reel

Blooper Reel

Blooper Reel

Blooper Reel

Blooper Reel

I MADE IT HOME

I just wanted to let you know that
I made it home.

Everything is so pretty here,
so white, so fresh, so new.
I wish that you could close
your eyes so you could see it too.

Please try not to be sad for me.
Try to understand.
God is taking care of me...
I'm in the shelter of His hands.

Here there is no sadness,
and no sorrow, and no pain.
Here there is no crying,
and I'll never hurt again.

Here it is so peaceful,
when all the angels sing.
I really have to go for now ...
I've just got to try my wings.

Made in the USA
Columbia, SC
10 December 2024

0b064876-8c37-4cc3-b99c-711e07745f90R01